T0118417

Intwasa
Poetry

Intwasa
Poetry

edited by
Jane Morris

'amaBooks

ISBN 978-0-7974-3645-9
EAN 9780797436459

©This collection: 'amaBooks, 2008

©Each contribution remains the copyright of the author

Published by 'amaBooks
P.O. Box AC1066, Ascot, Bulawayo
email: amabooks@gator.co.zw
www.amabooksbyo.com

Typeset by 'amaBooks
Printed by Automation Business Forms, Bulawayo

Cover Paintings: Aubrey Bango

Cover design: Veena Bhana

'amaBooks would like to express their thanks to
SABDET for making this publication possible and to
Alliance Française de Bulawayo for their continuing
support.

No part of this publication may be reproduced, stored in
a retrieval system, or transmitted in any form or by any
means, electronic, mechanical, photocopying, recording
or otherwise, without the prior permission of the
publisher.

Contents

Foreword

Bulawayo's premier arts festival, the Intwasa Arts Festival koBulawayo, is held in September each year – it is spring, *intwasa* in the SiNdebele language. Spring is the time in western Zimbabwe when flowers begin to grace the thirsty land, a time that heralds the coming of the summer and the longed for rains, a time for a new beginning.

The Intwasa Arts Festival koBulawayo showcases a wide range of the arts, including literary arts. In the short period since the first Intwasa Festival in 2005, the literary arts sector has grown to become one of the leading literary events in the region. And one of the most anticipated components of literary arts has been poetry. Writers from outside Zimbabwe have played a significant role in developing poetry at the festival: Owen Sheers and Lloyd Robson from Wales, Véronique Tadjo from Côte D'Ivoire, and Joelle Taylor from England. Equally important have been the award-winning Zimbabwean writers and poets who have taken part: Julius Chingono, Chirikure Chirikure, John Eppel, Ignatius Mabasa, Deon Marcus and Albert Nyathi.

It is these poets who are featured in this collection, together with several of the local poets who have made poetry at Intwasa such a success: Shepherd Mandhlazi, Judy Maposa, Mthabisi Phili, and John Simcoe Read.

I must also mention the role that 'amaBooks Publishers have made in Intwasa Literary Arts. They have been closely involved in the organization of each of the festivals, have launched several books during them, encouraged local writers to continue in these difficult times and have worked closely with other sectors in the festival.

This anthology is concrete testimony to the positive fruits that follow creative interactions between artists from very different cultures and traditions. It demonstrates that there is a promise of a brighter future in the arts for our city and for Zimbabwe. This is the promise that is enshrined and encapsulated in the spirit of Intwasa.

Pathisa Nyathi.
Chair
Board of the Intwasa Arts Festival koBulawayo.

Julius Chingono

About words

Listen with care
slippery words
slide away with the air.

Talk with care
slippery words
slip off the tongue.

Handle with care
this side up
contains words.

Stand well away
falling words
when mouths open.

Ditched

She had spent the night
alone
again.
It dawned in her mind
he was not returning
to her.
Dawn melted into tears
brushed away with speed
hidden from her baby
who had just learnt
to pronounce, Daddy.

Half Mast

Some national flags
prefer
to fly at half mast
are ashamed
of what they behold
from high up
at full mast.
Often they coil
around the post
in sheer disgust
when at full mast.

It denotes

If you walk by
and find me
lying on my side, curled
like a comma
with no blanket
to cover myself
I am not in a coma
it denotes –
stop briefly
and ponder over these times.

If you find me
lying on my side
legs stretched straight
head and shoulders
bent forwards towards my loins
like a question mark
it denotes –
provide explanations
why certain people
happen to sleep
on street pavements.

If you find me
lying on my back
my whole body stretched
at horizontal attention
like an exclamation mark
it denotes –
I am in shock
do not bother
I will recover.

And when you find me
coiled
my head between my legs
round like a full stop
it denotes –
stop and tender first aid
subject freezing.

They are picked

They are picked
maimed by mines
crossing borders
from troubled nations.
They are picked across the border
murdered in the streets
where they are squatters.
They are picked
at boundaries
picked by flooded rivers
attempting to swim
across borders.
They are picked
by crocodiles
crossing borders
that are rivers.
They are picked
across the border
picking their lives
in trash bins
picking comfort
in drain pipes.
They are picked
in foreign lands
picketing host politicians
who cannot
accommodate them anymore.

Chirikure Chirikure

Dancing mother

that rugged, shrivelled woman
dancing with a vigorous smile
just for a cup or two of home brew
is my mother, beacon of my life

the IMF structured her dignity

Mutserendende

Every little boy in my village
Can describe with joy and pride
How you play the *mutserendende* game.
You chop a healthy *munhanzva* tree
Cut the branches off the stem
Then drag the log up a mountain.

Like Jesus Christ on a donkey
You mount the log, holding tight
Then, whoosh, you zoom down.

It's so fast and furious
Eyes closed, breath held
You surrender all to fate.

You land with a big thud
Your backsides tattered
Bleeding in hot ecstasy.

So do many among us
Leading life fast and furious
Landing with tattered, bleeding souls.

Time to move on

Sitting in the white wintry sun
Watching birds winging in total peace
The mind switches to one's bare feet:
        Two feet
           Lucky to still have them both
        Ten toes
           Blessed to still have them all.

Who made that stupendous blunder?
The feet, straying in the wrong area?
The mouth, blurting the wrong party slogan?

Wrong area?
        Who decides that?
Party slogan?
        Who designs that?

Two feet
For perfect mobility
Ten toes
For total balance.

Time to move on
Where the feet's heart desires.

John Eppel

Border Jumping

Once all set about with fever trees
where hippos squeaked like rubber toys
and crocs gave rides to girls and boys:
the Limpopo River, if you please.

Now the banks are greasy with leftovers:
a doek, a hair extension, a knitted
bootie (pink for girls), a broken sandal.

In the high and far-off times, the croc
he lengthened the elephant's nose,
vamped it from a boot to a hose,
stretched it to a stocking from a sock.

Now a decayed, half-eaten corpse, grey-green,
lies unidentified near the bottly
tree with eight leaves only, and twisty roots.

Once long ago in colonial times
they lied to us in clever rhymes;
now the truth is the biggest lie,
so we cross the Limpopo, and die.

Giving

When the mbira plays,
the tree's sap stirs;
from its cave in the hills
a leopard purrs.

When the mbira plays,
a boulder shifts;
and dust from the pathway
through sunlight sifts.

When the mbira plays,
a hornbill cries;
a baby is born and
a baby dies.

When the mbira plays,
she gives, then gives;
something in me goes dead
and something lives.

When the mbira plays,
the tree's sap spills;
on a track in the grass
a leopard kills.

My Home Town

The kites, I notice, are keeping away,
the night adders have absented themselves,
the hedgehogs are taking a holiday,
and the geckoes have deserted the shelves.

Where are the abdim storks of yesteryear
that stalked the playing fields of Milton School?
Where are those creatures that all schoolboys fear:
water scorpions in the swimming pool?

The bees have packed their bags and buzzed away,
the button spiders have excused themselves,
the toads have gone for a year and a day,
woodwasps have evacuated the shelves.

Only rats and flies and people remain,
and cockroaches, and killer germs that grow
and grow like footprints down memory lane,
in the City of Kings: Bulawayo.

Shards

In a low country clear of the hills,
near where the Shashani River spills
in a good season – discovered there,
Early Stone Age tools, hand-axes, rare
now that plunderers, from the Trekker
(known to his foes as Ndaleka),
through the likes of Carl Mauch, Thomas Baines,
to Cecil John Rhodes and other stains
of imperial ink, have come and gone,
some under the ground and some upon.

Rare too are the human bits that in
more recent times, still adorned with skin,
in that low country of thorns and spines,
just clear of the hills, long worked-out mines
like Antelope, there discovered,
dropped down abandoned shafts and covered
with leafy branches, clumps of grass, stones,
because the police have moved the bones,
some muscle still attached to a groin,
and a 1980 five cent coin.

Waiting

I count the falling frangipani leaves.
Early April, the nights are growing cold;
the scent of wood smoke sours as neighbours burn
their household rubbish; every now and then
a discarded aerosol can explodes
triggering memories of another time,
another place, another war.

So quickly do they change from fluid green
to yellowish, to desiccated brown;
and yet, the drop, the clatter, ages takes;
takes ages: either way.   In terminal
cymes some flowers remain, as white as wax,
mingling the bitter sweets of paradise
with odours of anxiety.

Like sharpening blades on steel the plovers cry
as homeless people wander near their nests
waiting for news, waiting for results.   Who
will it be?   These falling leaves remind me
that the day has come and gone for ballots
to be counted, results announced, and I'm
afraid that change will never come.

Ignatius Mabasa

Epitaph

We silently walk to the cemetery
We, pallbearers of our own coffin.

We used to have a life
And an economy
Running on dollars and sense.

Now we are a graveyard
Full of shallow graves
Mounds of fresh earth
And crooked stick crosses.

Ravens disembowel corpses
Singing a harsh type of dirge
No dignity, no rites, no tears
No pastor, no speech, no soil!

Ghetto Lights

Ghetto lights, aloof sentinels
Blink in horror seeing terror
Aborting girl, sticky blood
Waits, listens, shakes, waits
To sneak into the occupied loo
Where a lodger is peeing with
One hand holding the door shut.
Aborting girl, dry caking blood
Waits, listens, shakes, waits
Praying, let there be water
To send foetuses into oblivion…

Poetry

Poetry is an old man in dusty fields
A scarecrow, talking to himself
Poking the stunted rapoko crop
And asking himself
"What happened to the land
That the government redistributed?
Was it all taken by the news-reader
Because he got the news first?"

Shepherd Mandhlazi

When We Were Young

When we were young
Dusty and noisy
Sometimes nosy
Innocence epitomised?
When we were young
Bathing in muddy pools
Trapping tadpoles
Screaming like fools.
When we were young
Popcorn
Candy
No worry in the world.
When we were young
Did money grow on trees?
Were babies bought?
When we were young.

Judy Maposa

How about?

How about
A world of dreams fulfilled
Not one, or two, or three
But where one's cup is ever full?
Not
Babies crying
For a drop of milk
In this country of milk and honey
Corrupted, yielding hunger.
Not
Disillusioned youth
No faith in the future
No share in their sightless vision
Escaping our birthright to servitude and slavery.
Not
Hands outstretched, faces downturned
The wretched of the streets
Salting the earth with their tears
Waiting for those who please
to hear their pleas.
Not
Laws to oppress, curb every word
Thoughts panel-beaten, daring no dissent
Dreams in monochrome
Shunning the rainbow and the butterfly
So fragile our wings we fear death.

Not
Guns and wars talking for us
Greed a universal creed and money the god
Where the human has lost itself in the chase
Of elusive shadows that lead to more shadows
Vicious circles of use and abuse.
How about
A space for you, a place for me
To laugh and play and embrace
Telling our stories, dancing our lives
Looking back to say we have lived?

Deon Marcus

A Dialogue

He could not find a word to say,
 so gave his hand
 instead.

He could not find an answer,
 so shared a sigh
 instead.

He could not share his heart,
 so sent his soul
 instead.

He could not let himself,
 so dreamt a dream
 instead.

Love

Love is still that old and wrinkled hand,
so callused worn, so stiffly borne, yet which an-
other still can touch with a touch that's butterfly warm.

Root and Rain

From one to another,
from hand to hand, as two
made one, joined through the eye

of a ring;

let no man set apart,
or between it come, that in
the end the band will stretch to fit

the son.

There is something

in the sound of a closing door,
in the way a curtain draws, the blur of
a TV screen, in the warmth of a polished floor;

in the steam that mirrors frost,
in the dome of a fresh baked roll, the
sound of a clinking glass, in the shimmer of

a small brass bowl; in the root of
an age old tree, the onyx eye of a dove, the
worn out fingers of a glove, perhaps a shade of love?

The Unsown

The graves are young these days, dug
in hardened earth that all too quick resigns its
belly-stones, tempted by too sweet a barter-trade. For

little spent far more is gained, where
weeds were grown, far greater things are there
now sown. Yet, this garden will yield no blooms, nor fill

the air with fragrant scent, rather
keep cocoon-like held the seeds that there
now lie, and slow decay their dreams, undreamt.

Albert Nyathi

My Daughter

When I demand
That you be home before dark every day
I, my daughter, do not hate you dear
I am merely trying to protect you

From the claws of tigers
That love to feast in the dark
From the panting leopards
Stalking like ghosts
Almost ready to leap at you

I am merely trying to protect you
From hungry lions silently eyeing you
Licking their lips
Ready to pounce on you
From the jumpy jumpy monkeys
That move from tree to tree
From branch to branch
Without any particular base

I am trying to protect you
From the proud peacocks
That love to show off bales of dollars
And pound sterling notes
To their victims like you

When I say
Be home before dark every day
I am merely trying
To protect you, dear

From the trumpeting elephants
That love party times in the depth of the night
From scaly crocodiles
Whose mouths are always open wide
To welcome any visitor wandering about
In search of greener pastures in the dark

I am trying to protect you
From the seemingly innocent porcupine
That will rip your heart apart
Before you even reach its soul,
From jackals
Whose business it is to ensure
Innocent souls like you
Live ever to regret all their lives

I am trying to protect you
From giraffes that look down on you
And will take you on
Right from the top
Down to the bottom
From the puff adder whose tongue is always sweet
With venom

I am merely being dutiful as a father
It is my duty to protect you
From black mambas that hate to miss a target
From the hyenas whose mouths are always watering

I am trying to protect you dear daughter

From the concerned social doctors
Who are only ready to operate on you
Deep in the secret of the night

They all want to win your heart,
And remember the python preys on its victim
By changing colours
O, those rainbow colours
Aren't they beautiful?

But remember they all are meant
To rip your heart apart!
Daughter, take heed, darkness has no eyes.

St. Valentine's Day

I hate flowers on 14 February
Every day must be St. Valentine's Day
Flowers wither and must be renewed every day
Love withers and must be renewed every day
I hate roses on St. Valentine's Day.

Struggles

They crush
The tired souls
The cheated
The robbed
The discouraged
The discontented
But still dawn will break!

Pathisa Nyathi

Upon Mzilikazi Bridge

The sprawling dusty townships
Come into foggy focus
Matshobana, Entumbane, Mpopoma.
Blue smoke lazily mingles
With choking dust from bare streets
Both twirl and waft above
The architectural monotony of dreary houses
Finally adding more layers of sordid grime
To drooping leaves that long lost their shine
Like the beleaguered residents
Who can no longer afford *lifebuoy* soap
Or the *nivea* cream of the cross border trader.

The road to town entraps many a car
Through a kaleidoscope of crumbling potholes
Enduring motifs of these hard times.
Tall brown grass laces road verges
An ideal rendezvous for mating rodents
And a hideout for part-time township lovers.

A silent absence pervades the service station
A white elephant that never sees a car
A facility offering no service, no refuge
Save for a solitary guard, *umawobho*
Who specializes in imaginative snoozing
And gazing at the erratic traffic lights
That control little traffic.

Beyond the rogue robots
Police maintain a toll-gate of visible corruption
Squeezing hard cash out of hapless commuter crews
Who dare not challenge law and authority
Lest their death-traps are taken off the road
For safekeeping at the local VID.

Township folk converge here
Where they safely cross the railway line
As they trudge and slog into town
Their holed shoes showcasing sockless feet
Their tired togs telling tales of abject poverty
Their surly looks of agony and torment
The easterly wind desiccating their ashen faces.

"Our people are a resilient people
Who will never yield to imperial pressure
Who will never surrender to neo-colonialism
We walked from Mozambique
We certainly can walk into town
Forward with the revolution!"

Below the bridge the freedom train comes racing by
Passengers jostling and shoving
Hoping to get a breath of air
Only to get wafts of stink from Mazayi Spruit
Notorious for its reeking stench
Worse than the farted air from a famished skunk.

From the bridge cooling towers loom large
They ran out of steam a long while ago
As have the scruffy glue-sniffing street kids.
Smog and smoke from early morning fires
Fill the tear-welling eyes of township dwellers
Impairing their vision of the present and the future.

Mthabisi Phili

Sunset in Mzilikazi

Soft and warm as in the arms of a loving man,
it has calmed down now.
Grasses share secrets for the last time,
the sun's shutters, shamed, shy away.
Workers cycle home over the bridge on Luveve Road,
windows blink constantly, their eyes now heavy with
fatigue.
The Mayadi sings praises for this safe day
but the fool retires without a prayer.
Sunset in Mzilikazi:
beautiful dusk approaches;
all the season's maize with a fresh glow;
the trees bend once more to the light kisses of the sun.
all's in place now, no need to strive for love;
children's songs sound warmly;
nothing drags – all the birds fly smoothly home.
Women cymbal pots and pans;
good children do their work for school.
Dusky sun, hide to take off your soiled dress;
long have we shone and played together –
we for tomorrow's wedding need not be shy
but shine again, after tonight's bath.
So much for the violence of words.
Of course some will lurk in the shades of the night
to defraud the starry sky,
while lovers embrace under the red blanket.
Sunset in Mzilikazi:
Soft and warm as in the arms of a loving man.

John S. Read

Small House Bliss

We have	We will be
borrowed	patient
time to teach	pressing
each other	giving
our art of love	succulent
When we step	becoming full
aside this space	of thought
each room	that slowly fills
entwined with lust	to exultation

Until time's lease is spent   In pharmaceutical bliss

Lloyd Robson

calling planet woman

you ask i respond to big ideas
hunt galaxies
dodge dark matter
avoid gravitational collapse and cometary coma
spike the surrounding gas clouds
delve the coalsack nebula
in search of what
i no longer figure.

all i figure:

my head is pitch and you are bold
your dynamic deliverance and emergence from cluster
offers time dilation, energy emission, bright light in all
                                                    transmissions
your data rate burns my system and gives me space
to feel and consider

you are flare star and fireball
you create atmosphere within which
i explore
recover
and resolve personal dilemma
and if i'm lucky
evolve

for CF

bap-bah!

there ain't much to beat the
reassurance ov the
BOOM BOOMah! ov ya
nextdoor neighbah's orgaz(jaz)**m-hmm**
cuming thru the wall
reminding you
YOW!
AH!
life go**oohs** on
so why not **GET DOWN!**
(yes!
hammer
&
tongs)
I means:
bap-bah!
they'r getting it, in'ay?

get on
get on

bang the merry mortar
outa
the other side **ah!**
this wall

bang the merry mortar
out this wall

bap-bah!
bap-bah!

get on
get on...

hoover haiku

so firm the suction
so many attachments – ah!
empty hamster cage

this sticky heat

cornhead primed, the wheatsheaf tide laps cliffhigh
in milky wet sunshine at the edge of field.

laid under bramble hedge, i roll pert blackberries between
my teeth
project with my tongue & pop between your waiting lips.

over walnutwood eyes you drop your lids
loll fruit flesh & squeeze for release, suck juice, swallow
pips.

we kiss, join & rejoice in the field off the gulling sea,
reverberate the low breeze
the pumping thud of human blood, quiverheavy with salt
& seed.

our sweated sighs entwine with the bush branch & leaf,
the final flicked wingbeats
of blacksaffron bees prone on the sandy mud, each
bleached with this sticky heat.

when she sleeps

& when she sleeps

she hears warpt floorboards creak
feels draught of lift cover
me settling in

sees thro lids lite hazing
peers, smiles
feels me
reach.

& when she sleeps

i read outloud 'trout fishing in america'
to lull her dreams

she keeps arms under covers
her chin
the quilt
two fists

we meet our cheeks
& warmth sticks

she turns
& kisses

she rolls from me

uniformly i follow
take up

her space
stretch warm where she's been
allow
no release.

& when she sleeps

in the fleshfolds of nite
where my thumb fits the fob of her concave waist
holsters her gunbelt
my elbow to hip...

& when she sleeps

she tries to turn back to me

i sleep
i flail
rage continuous
or
deadweight

she soothes my outbursts til i too sleep quietly
tho i battle my dreams
she sleeps again
instantly.

& when she sleeps

me
& the cat
orbit her shape

she
radiates

offers
no resistance
to proximity.

& when she sleeps

i long to disturb her
tranquillity

plan to eat gratefully

her

cum breakfast

Owen Sheers

The Equation

He told me how, after soft afternoons
teaching logarithms and waving away
the blackboard's hieroglyphics with a damp cloth,
he'd return home to the sweet methane of the chicken
                                                    sheds.

How he'd change from his suit into overalls
and how he dug his hand deep into the bucket
to draw out a leaking fist, which he opened,
a sail of grain unfurling to the birds beneath.

And how later that same hand would flatten
to find a way through the dark
under the sleeping weight of a hen, to bring out,
like a magician whose tricks are just the way of things,

one egg, warm and bald in his brown palm.

Not Yet My Mother

Yesterday I found a photo
of you at seventeen,
holding a horse and smiling,
not yet my mother.

The tight riding hat hid your hair,
and your legs were still the long shins of a boy's.
You held the horse by the halter,
your hand a fist under its huge jaw.

The blown trees were still in the background
and the sky was grained by the old film stock,
but what caught me was your face,
which was mine.

And I thought, just for a second, that you were me.
But then I saw the woman's jacket,
nipped at the waist, the ballooned jodhpurs,
and of course the date, scratched in the corner.

All of which told me again,
that this was you at seventeen, holding a horse
and smiling, not yet my mother,
although I was clearly already your child.

The Umbilical Tree

I explain.

I have come to find my umbilical tree,
the tree that holds my root in its roots.

She pinches my cheek,
shifts her crossed legs on the floor of someone else's
                                                  house,
all these years and still someone else's house.

The sun halves itself in the sea.

I explain.

You are Lor who looked after me,
you buried it here,
after I was born.

You told my parents I would never
forget my roots.
I have not forgotten.

She explains.

She is in someone else's house,
all these years and still someone else's house,
and the tree is gone, plucked by a hurricane years ago.

She says she saw it go, taken like a match in the wind,
that nothing was left,
just a perfect belly button of dark brown soil.

Valentine

The water torture of your heels
emptying before me down that Paris street,
evacuated as the channels of our hearts.

That will be one memory.

The swing of the tassels on your skirt
each step filling out the curve of your hip;
your wet lashes, the loss of everything we'd learnt.

That will be another.

Then later – holding each other on the hotel bed
like a pair of wrecked voyagers
who had thought themselves done for,

only to wake washed up on the shore
uncertain in their exhaustion
whether to laugh or weep.

That my valentine, will be the one I'll keep.

When You Died

I ran to the top of a hill
and sat on its broken skull
of stone and wind-thinned soil.
I watched the Black Mountains darken
and the river slip the grip of the town.

I went to the pond,
the one in the field above the house,
its borders churned to mud by the cattle.
I thought of how we skated there,
taking the risk, despite the sound of the ice,
creaking like a boat's wet rigging.

I went to your house,
and saw the long, low chicken sheds.
I remembered your voice behind me,
as I, afraid of the sudden peck,
stretched my hand into the dark
to take the warm eggs, one of them
wearing a feather.

Véronique Tadjo

The cries from under the earth

1

SHOW HER
THE CRIES FROM UNDER THE EARTH
THE OPPRESSIVE SUMMERS
DEVASTATING RAINS
TEACH HER
TO HOLD HER BREATH
TO THE BEAT OF THE FIRST LEAVES
HOLD ONTO HER HAND
TO THE VERY END OF THE PATH
LET HER CONQUER HER OWN FEAR!

2

TELL HER
THE VICTORIES TALLIED
AND THE PATHWAYS OF NOON.
TELL HER TOO
OF THE GLIMMERS OF EARLY MORNING
AND THE HEART POUNDING
THERE IS NO
MOON WITHOUT A WAKING
NO SONG
WITHOUT A TOURACO*.

47

3

SING TO ME
THE STORY
OF THE PLOUGHMAN
HIS SEARING SWEAT
AND THE TOO-RED EARTH
TALK TO ME
ABOUT THE WOMAN
WITH HEAVY BREASTS
AND BELLY-GOURD
IN THE INTENSE FURNACE
OF A NIGHT WITHOUT TOMORROW
TEACH ME
THE CLOSED BOOKS
AND REACHING HANDS
THE HOPES BROKEN
IN THE BLACK OBLIVION
OF A GAUDY LITTLE TOWN.

4

YOU THE TRASH PICKERS
THE HOBBLED
WITH FILTHY STUMPS
THE ONE-EYED
THE CRAWLERS
YOU THE SCAVENGERS
THE SLUM URCHINS
I SALUTE YOU.

5

WHAT BURDEN DO YOU BEAR
IN THIS FOUL WORLD
HEAVIER THAN THE CITY
DYING OF ITS WOUNDS?
WHAT POWER
LINKS YOU TO THIS FRIGID EARTH
THAT BIRTHS TWINS
ONLY TO SEPARATE THEM?
THAT RAISES BUILDINGS
ONLY TO CRUSH YOU
UNDER TONS OF CEMENT
AND STEAMING ASPHALT?

6

YOU THE DEVOURERS
OF SCRAPS
THE HOMELESS
THE SHELTERLESS
WHAT GAZE DO YOU LEVEL
ON THE HORIZON IN FLAMES?

*Touraco - a bird from the north of Côte d'Ivoire

Joelle Taylor

Mother's Milk

My mother has breast cancer
Breast cancer has my mother
The life giver
Has turned upon her.

The breast
Bit
Back.

We follow in our mother's footsteps
Not our father's.

The thin black spider
Squats at the spiny top
And suckles the milk
Before it can
Succour her children
And this spider
Corrupt
Fingering lymph-like worry beads
Feeds
And grows still thinner
On our future.

And now the veins
Of her empty breasts

Envelopes without letters
Are clogged with litter
Her shelves are empty
Children
Queue.

It spreads
Its insectile legs
Like the sickly roots
Of a needy tree
Until they
Become her veins
Her streets
That we once kicked and scuffed
Are now dust
And useless air.

The life giver
Has turned upon her.

I have hurt my heart mum
See?
It bleeds.

My mother is dying
But still she breathes
Denies
Knits
Reads
As her breast
Bites back
And from our
Beautiful future
Feeds.

The Navigator

Keisha
Was the kind of girl who left lights on.

Who walked into walls –
Spilled her smile down the shrug of her shirt
Stumbled into furniture
Like it was her future.

Never did quite fit her body.

Clumsy.

Keisha!
Will you look where you're going!

Well

She knew where she was going alright
Just didn't much appreciate the view
Didn't much appreciate the navigator
Started to seek alternative routes.

For a clumsy girl
She has a steady hand.

She has sketched a map of herself
On skin stretched tight as fathers' fists
Tracing the long walk home
On the back of her hand
Inner arm
Wrist.

Lines of latitude and longitude.

She scratches herself.
A 13 year itch
She scratches herself.
Thin. Red. Mother. Lips.
Rattles the bars of her rib cage
And marks off the days
Until she is 16
When she will draw a thin red line through her skin
Proof marks in the margin of her life
And she will
Begin
Again.

Because
When he opened the pages of her blouse like it was a
                                        well-read book
He changed the story –
Half-written first draft.
Keisha has her name engraved in gilt
Along the stutter of her spine
Keisha
Volume One
Underlined

But
When he did that thing
And that thing did her
Keisha ceiling clinging
Realised the possibilities
Because if he could change the story
Erase the topography
Half way through
Then. So. Could. She.

Today
Keisha
Is the kind of girl who walks upright
Who walks in spite
Who carries full friendships in the pockets of her
favourite jeans
Who travels her body like an unexplored land
Because today
Keisha is the kind of girl who is
Frankly
A
Woman.

No Man's Land/ No Land's Man

His face was a foreign country
And his tongue was a concealed gun
His laugh was an air raid siren
And his mouth was a deep cave dug in Iraqi earth
His beard was a barbed wire fence between borders
And his skin was a hand-written map sewn into his shirt
His eyes were abandoned landmines
And his voice was radio static caught between stations
His ribs were the gripped bars of a Guatanamo cage
And his toes were rows of roadside graves
His pleading hands were opposing peoples
And his veins were dusty tributaries clogged with rusting
cars
And he walked like a school child in the rubble of his home
And he spoke like a low-flying plane looking to land
Welcome.
To
England.
And he belonged here
And should have stayed here.
But immigration central was a love letter written in another
language
And when he smiled
His teeth
Were the New York
Skyline.

Contributors

Julius Chingono was born on a commercial farm in 1946, and has worked for most of his life on the mines as a blaster. He has had his poetry published in several anthologies of Shona poetry, including *Nhetembo*, *Mabvumira eNhetembo* and *Gwenyambira*, between 1968 and 1980. His only novel, *Chipo Changu*, was published in 1978, an award-winning play, *Ruvimbo*, was published in 1980, and a collection of poetry and short stories, *Not Another Day*, in 2006. His poetry in English has also been published in South African and Zimbabwean anthologies.

Chirikure Chirikure, born in Gutu in 1962, is best known as one of Zimbabwe's most talented performance poets. His first book of poetry, *Rukuvhute*, received honourable mention in the 1990 Noma Awards and was followed by *Chamupupuri* and *Hakurarwi, We Shall not Sleep*. Chirikure performs his poetry in Shona and in English and usually performs with musician Chiwoniso Mararire and also with DeteMbira, an mbira band of which he was a founding member. Much of his poetry has been recorded in audio form, and he and the DeteMbira band have produced one album, *Napukeni*.

John Eppel's first novel, *D.G.G. Berry's The Great North Road*, won the M-Net Prize in South Africa. His second novel, *Hatchings*, was chosen for the series in the Times Literary Supplement on the most significant books to have come out of Africa. His first book of poems, *Spoils of War*, won the Ingrid Jonker Prize. His other novels, *The Giraffe Man*, *The Curse of the Ripe Tomato* and *The Holy Innocents*, and his poetry anthologies *Sonata for Matabeleland*, *Selected Poems: 1965-1995* and *Songs My Country Taught Me* have received critical acclaim. His recent collections of short stories and poems are *The Caruso of Colleen Bawn and Other Short Writings* and *White Man Crawling*. His new novel *The English Teacher* is to be published soon.

Ignatius Tirivangani Mabasa started off as a poet before venturing into prose. His poetry has appeared in the anthologies *Tipeiwo Dariro* and *Muchinokoro Kunaka*. He has written two novels in Shona, *Mapenzi (Fools)* and *Ndafa Here?* His debut novel *Mapenzi* won first prize in the Zimbabwe Book Publishers' Association Awards in 2000 and was subsequently nominated as one of Zimbabwe's 75 Best Books of the century. His short stories have appeared in *Writing Now* and in *Short Writings from Bulawayo III*. Married to Conelia, they have two sons.

Shepherd Mandhlazi was born in Bulawayo, and grew up in Mutare. He taught English language, integrated science and biology courses for several years until he left in 2004 to pursue a career in the arts. Shepherd is now a playwright, filmmaker, poet and commentator based in Bulawayo.

Judy Maposa was born in Bulawayo in 1972, and at an early age would lose herself in a world of words and imagination in the Tshabalala library. The eldest child of a family of seven she lived for some time in the early 80's in her rural Gwanda home, which nurtured a deep love for the open spaces and rocky heights of natural Zimbabwe. She is a former journalist and temporary Festival Co-ordinator of Intwasa Festival, but now has her own company, Art Connexion.

Deon Marcus was born in Bulawayo in 1978. He has studied Accounting Science, Classical Studies and Ancient History, as well as piano and viola. Deon has had poems published in the three anthologies of *Short Writings from Bulawayo* and his collection of poetry, *Sonatas*, was launched at Intwasa 2005. *Sonatas* went on to win a National Arts Merit Award as well as the 2005 Zimbabwe Book Publishers Association Award for best poetry or drama.

Albert Nyathi is a performance dub-poet. He started fusing his written poems with music so as to blow life into them, to blow life into dead words. He has performed in many countries throughout the world and has released several CDs. He has released a DVD, recorded live in Durban, the UK and Zimbabwe, titled *The World As We Dance Along*. Albert won the Zimbabwe National Poetry Award in 1995 and his poetry collection, *Echoes of Zimbabwe*, is to be published in 2008.

Pathisa Nyathi was born in Sankonjana, Kezi. After a career in education and public relations, he is now a cultural and historical consultant. Pathisa is a published poet, playwright, historian and biographer; his most recent publications include *In Search of Freedom: Masotsha Ndlovu, Material Culture of the AmaNdebele, Izibongo Lezangelo ZamaNdebele kaMzilikazi, Alvord Mabena: the Man and his Roots, Traditional Ceremonies of the AmaNdebele* and *Zimbabwe's Cultural Heritage*. He is a columnist for several newspapers and magazines, and is Chair of the Board of the Intwasa Arts Festival koBulawayo.

Mthabisi Phili is an artist and poet based at the National Gallery of Zimbabwe in Bulawayo. He has exhibited with the Visual Artists Association of Bulawayo since 2003 and is a visual arts consultant for the Intwasa Arts Festival. Mthabisi has read his poetry at Bulawayo Poetry Circle meetings and at each Intwasa Festival.

John Simcoe Read was born in Harare and has lived in Mashonaland and Midlands as part of farming communities. He trained in Pietermaritzburg, Cape Town and Oxford. He joined the National University of Science and Technology in Bulawayo from the University of Zimbabwe as Professor of Applied Biology and Biochemistry in 2000 and since then has learnt a lot more about the culture, the history and the personal tragedies of Matabeleland. John has had poems published in each of the *Short Writings from Bulawayo* collections.

Lloyd Robson is a poet, novelist, broadcaster, workshop tutor, freelance book designer/typesetter and editor. Lloyd often works abroad and in recent years has worked in Australia, Europe, India, Japan, Sierra Leone, Zimbabwe and the USA. He divides his time between Cardiff and New York and leads a creative writing project in Sömmerda, Germany, every July. He has written commissioned documentary scripts for BBC Wales TV and BBC Radio Four. His most recent publication is *Oh Dad! A Search for Robert Mitchum*.

Owen Sheers was born in Fiji in 1974 and brought up in South Wales. The winner of an Eric Gregory Award and the 1999 Vogue Young Writer's Award, his first collection of poetry, *The Blue Book*, was short-listed for the Welsh Book of the Year and the Forward Prize Best 1st Collection. His debut prose work *The Dust Diaries*, a non-fiction narrative set in Zimbabwe, was short-listed for the Royal Society of Literature's Ondaatje Prize and won the Welsh Book of the Year 2005. In 2004 he was selected as one of the Poetry Book Society's 20 Next Generation Poets. Owen's second collection of poetry, *Skirrid Hill* won a 2006 Somerset Maugham Award. He is also a playwright and his first novel, *Resistance*, was published in 2007.

Véronique Tadjo is an author and painter from Côte D'Ivoire. She has won several literary awards including Le Grand Prix d'Afrique Noire in 2005. Véronique has written many books, but is perhaps best known for her book on the Rwandan genocide, *The Shadow of Imana, Travels in the Heart of Rwanda* and for *As the Crow Flies*. She has been a judge for the Caine Prize for African Writing and for the European Union Literary Prize for South African writing. She is currently the Head of French Studies at the University of Witswatersrand in South Africa.

Joelle Taylor is a poet, award winning playwright and spoken word artist, as well as workshop facilitator. She has toured solo and as a member of Atomic Lip. Joelle also writes performance novels, including *Whorror Stories I* and *II*, and is Artistic Director of Transgressive Art Physical Poetry Company. She was UK Performance Poetry Slam Champion in 2000, and hosts Mother Foucault Spoken Word Burlesque in Covent Garden, London. Her book *Lesbians Talk Violent Relationships* was published in 1995.

Acknowledgements

Not Yet My Mother, *The Umbilical Tree* and *When You Died*, by Owen Sheers, were previously published in *The Blue Book*, Seren, 2000, *The Equation* and *Valentine* in *Skirrid Hill*, Seren, 2005. Copyright © 2005 Owen Sheers. Reproduced by permission of the author c/o Rogers, Coleridge & White Ltd., 20 Powis Mews, London W11 1JN. This work is copyright and has been recorded for the sole use of people with print disabilities. No unauthorised broadcasting, public performance, copying or re-recording is permitted.

when she sleeps, by Lloyd Robson, was previously published in *Poetry Wales*, 2001; *Fire*, 2002; *bbboing!*, Parthian, 2003. *bapbah!* and *hoover haiku* were also published in *bbboing!*

The cries from under the earth, by Véronique Tadjo, contains excerpts from *Red Earth*, translated by Peter S. Thompson, Eastern Washington University Press, 2005. *Red Earth* was originally published in French as *Laterite*.

My Daughter, *St. Valentine's Day* and *Struggles*, by Albert Nyathi, are to appear in *Echoes from Zimbabwe*, ZPH, 2008

We acknowledge that several poems in the book have appeared on the Poetry International website and other websites.